THE LOVE STORY OF
PAPA AND MAMA KNOPP

Anne Coleman Knopp

Anne Coleman Knopp

First published by Dog Ear Publishing
4011 Vincennes Road
Indianapolis, IN 46268
www.dogearpublishing.net

ISBN: 978-1-4575-6374-4

This book is printed on acid free paper.
Printed in the United States of America

Chapter One

CHRISTINE FELT AT 27 that she would never be married. In the small town of Somerset, Kentucky in 1946, women of her age were called old maids, and she was a school teacher as well, which completed the stereotype. In November, Christine had prayed and told the Lord that she was willing to stay single if that would bring Him more glory, but she was also willing to be married if He would get more glory from that. While at Walter and Gertrude Evans' home in Louisville, Kentucky in January 1947, Christine was teased about two young men who were doing mission work in the mountains of Virginia. Their names were Paul Knopp and Morton Brown. In July at the Kentucky State camp meeting, Christine was trying to get an evangelist to come to Somerset in the fall for two weeks of meetings. All of the evangelists she tried were booked up. Gertrude Evans told Christine privately that she had met Paul Knopp and was praying that she would meet him, fall in love, and marry him. Two couples who knew Paul and knew of Morton suggested that she write to them and see if they would consider coming. So she did, and they came to Somerset on September 13 and went to the room reserved for them. The next morning they went to the church and were already in the young people's class when Christine arrived.

She sat down by Mary Flynn and asked her, "Which one is which?"

"I think the tall one is Paul Knopp and the short one is Morton Brown," Mary said. Christine thought to herself, "It would be the short one I'd fall for if I fell for either one." Mary had their names mixed up!

Christine was praying, "Lord, don't let me fall in love with either of these young men. But Sunday night, just before she got in bed, while she was praying it seemed like the Lord said, "What about that prayer you prayed about me getting you a husband if I want you to get married?" Here she was praying against her own prayer. So she said, "Have your way, Lord!" Monday night after the service she invited them to come and eat lunch with her at the school where she taught. On Tuesday when Paul walked into the lunchroom, her heart did a little flip and she knew she could fall in love with him! The message he gave when it was his turn to speak was inspiring, and he had a way of speaking about life in Christ as a real relationship with someone who was closer than a brother. He urged the people to "break up your fallow ground", citing Jeremiah 4:3, when the Lord had spoken to his people through Jeremiah saying, "Break up your fallow (unplowed) ground, and do not sow among thorns." He also said "be fertile ground", citing the parable of the sower from Luke 8. He said when seed fell on good soil in the parable, meaning when people who had prepared their hearts before God through repentance and prayer heard the words of God, the seed came up and yielded a crop, a hundred times more than was sown. The seed on good soil stands for those with a noble and good heart, he told them, who by persevering produce a crop. His face glowed with hope and joy as he spoke of his Savior and Lord. He told them that the Lord is sowing the seed. The people were stirred by this message, and wanted to hear more. Christine had never heard anyone preach like this, and she was deeply impressed.

Her father had invited the young men to lunch on Sunday after the church service. If Paul was attracted to her, he didn't show it. He was friendly to everyone and interested in everyone. As the days of his visit passed, there were many opportunities to spend time together, especially since she was the church secretary and involved in all the youth activities. Everyone liked him and sought him out to spend time with him. After Paul and Christine had known one another for a few weeks and had spent a lot of time together, they were sitting with a map spread out on their laps. Paul reached under the map and held her hand. She had wondered if he had a sweetheart back home in Staunton, but when he did that, she knew he didn't. He just wasn't the kind of man to cheat, even by flirting.

The revival was creating a lot of interest and many people were attending, even from other churches. The meetings were every night, seven nights a week. The young people were especially excited about Paul and Morton's preaching, and a number of them asked if they could stay for a third week. The church pastor was an older gentleman, and his family wanted to move near Cincinnati, so some of the people of the church asked Paul if he would consider coming back to be the new pastor. They asked Christine as the church secretary to write a letter to Paul, inviting him formally to be their pastor. Christine felt as she typed it that her heart was glowing through every word. Paul accepted, and came back on October 22 to be the new pastor. Christine saw him at church on the night of the 23rd, and again felt such a stirring in her heart that it was hard to concentrate on the sermon.

Paul was staying in a rented room in a house down the hill from the church, and he had been sensing the same stirring of heart concerning Christine that she had about him. Morton had written a letter to Christine, but didn't mail it. In the letter, he said he wanted to show that the Lord sometimes reveals the future to people. He said that Christine and Paul would be married and he himself would be married to a girl from Staunton, Virginia, Paul's home town, before the end of that year. He mailed it after both weddings took place. Meanwhile, Paul said to himself, "If I'm going to marry Christine, then why am I sitting down here all by myself?"

On November 1, Paul brought a book on the works of John Bunyan to Christine's mother, Clara. Her mother's knees were locked in a sitting position due to the ravages of arthritis, and she was unable to walk. She wrote letters and did sewing, with Josephine, Christine's youngest sister, pedaling the Singer sewing machine with her hands as she sat on the floor. When Christine's mother Clara prayed for her children, she prayed that they would know the Lord as their Savior. She prayed the same for their spouses and their children and their children until Jesus would return to Earth. After Paul visited with her mother, Christine walked with him to the door. He said, "Christine, I'd like to come back sometime next week. I have a question to ask you." Christine had begun to hope that he loved her, and when he said this, she thought he was going to ask her to go home with him to Staunton for Christmas to meet his folks.

"How about asking me tonight?" she said boldly.

"Well, Okay, can we talk somewhere privately?" he asked.

So they went into the parlor, and she sat on the couch while he sat in a chair facing her.

"Have you ever thought of getting married?" he blurted out.

She sat back slightly, but hesitated only momentarily. "To you?" she asked.

"Yes, what do you think?"

This time she didn't hesitate. She had come to think of him as the only man she would ever love. "I think it would be about the most wonderful thing that could happen, except being a Christian." They talked awhile, adrift in the wonder of new love. Then she asked him when he was thinking to do it. He said he'd thought about Christmas. She said, "I'm off for Thanksgiving." He said that would be fine. They talked and laughed for an hour or so afterwards, and after he left, Christine wondered if it had been a dream. She had not expected such happiness to come into her life at this stage.

Chapter Two

CHRISTINE MARIE YAHNIG was the second child of her immigrant father's second wife. His first wife had given him two sons before she died. John Richard Yahnig, called Joe, had come over from Germany to this country with his parents before he was two. He married Christine's mother, Clara Moreland Simpson, from Ruth, KY and they lived on a farm. They raised corn, wheat, alfalfa, and cattle. Christine had an older brother, Richard, three younger brothers, Dudley, Albert, and Frank, and two younger sisters, Jessie and Josephine. When Christine was a little girl, Richard nicknamed her "Cricket" because she liked to hop from one stone to another on their flagstone walkway in front of the house. She was a tomboy and didn't enjoy dolls very much. She climbed trees and fell out of a tree one time. A stick stuck in her chest, but her mother removed it and she wasn't badly hurt, only scared. She also loved to read whenever she had free time. The farmhouse had no electricity and they heated with wood in fireplaces. There was a pot belly stove in the dining room for additional heat on special occasions, but for everyday meals, they ate in the kitchen. They had a telephone in the hallway with a hand crank. The family worked together and ate together. They liked Jell-O, but could only have it in winter because of the lack of a refrigerator to cool it in. In 1941 they got electricity, and it was such a novelty to the family that they were always experimenting. Now they could have Jell-O whenever they wanted, and a favorite dessert was different colors of Jell-O cut into squares and mixed up in a bowl with fruit. They froze fresh milk from their cows in ice trays and that was a special treat.

Christine liked washing clothes, and she used a washboard, wringing the water out of the clothes by hand. When she was growing up, they often had company and hosted visiting church speakers. She attended Lindsey Wilson Junior College and graduated in 1939. When Christine finished college, her family changed churches and started attending the Church of God, which was closer to home. She taught third grade in Ferguson for three years, then moved to fourth grade for four more years.

Paul had been born December 15, 1913 in Staunton, Virginia, at a house on 908 Trout Street. He was the oldest of eleven children, and he often worked in the garden at an early age. His siblings were Mark, James, Rebecca, Elizabeth, Hiram, Phillip, Anna Ruth, Dan, Simon, and Rhoda. The family were members of the United Brethren Church, but a new church came to town and their father, George, decided to join there instead. It was the Pilgrim Holiness Church. When Paul was ten years old, he attended a camp meeting on Montgomery Avenue. When they had an altar call, he went forward and gave his heart to the Lord. After that, he began to work with the youth in the church. George taught Sunday School and held a number of offices there, but after a time, he was disappointed in it because the people were so focused on outward appearance. He was a Bible student and taught some things that some of the people didn't like. The pastor suggested from the pulpit that he leave, and when Paul was twenty, the family complied. They had bought a large brick home on Middlebrook Avenue, and the basement held a large room. They began holding church meetings there, and about fifty people were attending. Paul had been studying the Bible with his father all his life, and so it was only natural that he would become one of the ministers. He had graduated from Lee High School and used a scholarship to attend Dunsmore Business College and study bookkeeping. He went there for two years and then started his first job, working as a secretary at JP Neff Orchard and earning $30 a month. Next he worked at Simmons Auto Parts for a short time and then became a secretary for a lawyer. This was during the Great Depression. Afterwards, he worked for Reid Brothers grocery and trucking. They sent him to the livestock market once a week.

Paul was drafted October 7, 1941. He prayed and asked the Lord what to do. He decided that he should sign up for alternative service. He was 27 years old, and later he found out that had he gone to the Army as a draftee, they would have sent him home as 4F due to his asthma, which had started when he was 15 years old. His brother was classified 4F for asthma, and his was not nearly as bad as Paul's. Paul went to North Carolina to help build the Blue Ridge Parkway with the Civilian Conservation Corps, or CCC. He worked with a group of men who made a line and passed rocks uphill to make the wall along the Parkway. The first night he didn't eat supper because he was so tired and he went straight to bed. His health improved during this time, and he took a Charles Atlas body building class. As a conscientious objector he got paid $5.00 a week.

Volunteers were called for to fight fires in California, and he signed up. Next he went to Oregon and drove a big CAT for awhile. He met a man named Morton Brown, a Quaker from New York, and together they started a Bible study. Paul had a furlough and he took a course from Fuller Seminary. He studied Isaiah, and it was his favorite book after that. One time they decided to cut each others hair in the camp. Paul was the "camp barber" after that. Paul had joined the CCC on October 7, and on December 7, the US got into the war. He stayed in for four years. Afterwards, Morton came with him to Staunton, saying he didn't know any Christians in New York. The two of them went to work for a year for an ornithologist in Goshen at Alum Springs. He asked them to organize his bird collection. He had lots of preserved birds in little drawers. Later the owner donated all the birds to Virginia Tech. Paul and Morton also began having Bible studies and camp meetings, and became rather popular in the area as speakers. It was around this time that Christine had written to him. When Paul first met her, the Lord spoke to him in a meeting and told him that she was going to be his wife.

Paul had waited until he was 34 to marry. His friend Carl Miller had tried to get him married. He had introduced him to the Church of God in Ashland, Kentucky. Carl said "Pick one out and I'll introduce you." Paul chose one, but she was already married, so Carl didn't introduce him to her. He didn't think too much about marriage otherwise. He had given a box of candy to a girl while he was in the service. She was a member of a different church, however, and didn't want to change churches. Paul didn't want to be tied down to a denomination, and also he didn't want to get married and attend a different church than his wife.

After asking Christine to marry him, Paul went to her father the next day to ask for her hand in marriage.

"You haven't known each other very long, but if you've made up your minds, I guess it's what you're going to do." Mr. Yahnig said.

Paul replied, "I'm willing to wait."

The older man was quiet for a minute, then said, "Go ahead." Paul said he would like to have his blessing, and he said he would give it. While Paul and her father were outside having this conversation, Christine asked her mother what they were talking about. Her mother looked at her quickly, and tears came immediately to her eyes. She had told her children that if they ever wanted to get married, not to hold back because of her disability. Four of her children were married within the next year. A couple of weeks after they got engaged, one night as Paul was saying goodnight, he asked Christine if he could kiss her.

"Yes, of course," and he did. That was their first kiss, and it was such a wonderful kiss that it confirmed to her all over again that he was the perfect man for her.

After they were engaged to be married, Paul and Christine started to date each other. In the next few days, whenever they shared their good news with anyone in the church, the person would say something like, "I've been praying and expecting this…I just didn't know it would be so soon." They planned the wedding for 4:30 in the afternoon on Thanksgiving Day. They didn't send invitations, but just announced it at church and asked everyone to come. Christine's brother Richard teased her that she'd be late for her own wedding, but she got there just in the nick of time. It was a very simple affair, with one attendant each for the bride and groom, and a few big ferns for decoration. Carl Miller, a pastor who had served with Paul in the conscientious objectors camps during the war, came from Louisville to perform the ceremony. Christine wore a white wool suit made for her for the occasion, and it was mid-calf length, so that she'd be able to get more wear out of it. She also wore a blouse crocheted by her mother. After she arrived at the wedding, Christine realized she hadn't lined anyone up to play piano, so she quickly found her cousin Pauline Grayson, who agreed and began playing the wedding march. One of Christine's friends, Marie Muse, sang the hymn, "Take my Life and Let it Be." Her sister Jessie took one picture on the front steps of the church after the ceremony. Paul had written to his family to tell them of the upcoming nuptials and to invite them to the wedding. His father wrote back that they'd be unable to attend, but "be sure to tell your bride what kind of family she is getting into."

For a honeymoon, the couple drove to Corbin, Kentucky and stayed in a hotel for one night. On the way there was a beautiful cloud with dark clouds on two sides and a bright silver streak in the middle. Christine thought, "In our life together there will always be a silver lining." The next day, they drove to Cumberland Falls and hiked around, then back to her parents for a week. While they were there, Christine's brother Dudley and his wife Alene were also visiting with their four-year-old son Carl and their twin baby girls, Carolyn and Marilyn.

Paul teasingly asked little Carl, "Could we have one of your baby sisters? You have two of them."

"No, you and Aunt Christine can go to the hospital and get your own," he stated.

Then the young couple moved into a trailer. Christine had never been in a trailer, but she was happy and fascinated with all the little cubbies and niches it held. They had bought furniture at Goldenberg Furniture store, and the store held it for them until they needed it. They lived there for several months. At Christmas, they traveled to Staunton so Paul's family could meet his bride. Paul had ten brothers and sisters, and though some of them had married and moved out by that time, there was still quite a welcoming committee. As the oldest son, Paul was welcomed home with open arms. His father worked at his own carpentry business, and had earned a reputation as a fine craftsman. Christine felt overwhelmed by them at first, because the people in her family were farmers and didn't have such a grand house, but they soon put her at ease.

Chapter Three

A FTER THE COUPLE returned to Kentucky, Paul was pastoring the family church, Somerset Church of God. Christine resigned her teaching job in January, 1948.

Her brother Albert had remarked, "My, Sis, with you teaching and him pastoring, you ought to make out good." She had started teaching in 1940 at a salary of $75 a month, and by now it had doubled to $150. Christine didn't want anyone to think they were "in it for the money." She resigned, and she always felt that was the right decision because she was free to visit people in the congregation as the pastor's wife.

One morning in July she thought she must be pregnant. She was eating peaches and a funny feeling came up in her throat. She told Paul she thought she was expecting a baby. They went to her parents' house for lunch that day.

"Pop, how'd you like to have a Knopp grandson?" she said to her father, Everyone was quiet; people didn't talk much about such things then.

After lunch, her mom said privately, "Honey, you shouldn't be talking like that, since you don't know for sure yet." That kept her quiet for awhile. It was two more months before she saw a doctor, but by then she was sure she was expecting. One night at church, she lost a little blood, and when she went to see her doctor, he said not to be on her feet a lot, and not to ride in the car a lot. She continued spotting off and on for about a month. This was worrying, but after praying a long time about it, she prayed, "Lord, if this child won't grow up to know you, just take it now. But if the child would honor you, let it live." She didn't want to bring a child into the world that wouldn't serve God. The spotting stopped.

In December, Paul became sick. His asthma had begun to get worse lately. They traveled to Staunton to visit his family, and he became very ill. He went to see the family physician, who told him that he had a bad case of tonsillitis.

Paul said, "But I had my tonsils removed when I was twelve!" The doctor replied that they must have grown back, because he had tonsils that were very inflamed. He suggested a change of climate and rest. Paul's parents suggested that they visit Paul's sister Libby and her husband Joe in San Antonio, Texas, where Joe was stationed in the Army. So to San Antonio they went. Paul resigned his pastorate in Somerset, Kentucky, and they moved to Texas.

The change in climate did seem to cause an improvement in Paul's health, and soon they began attending a Church of God there. The pastor immediately loved Paul and Christine, and asked Paul to be the youth pastor for the church. The youth group grew as a result, because the young people were drawn to him and brought their friends as well. Paul also began selling cars, and selling Fuller brushes in the business district. He found himself selling them mostly to the secretaries of businesses, and it soon became as much of a counseling ministry as a sales job. Everyone found him easy to talk with, and often people poured out their hearts and asked his advice on marriage and relationships. Paul had a saying that he was famous for, that people tended to think that marriage would be the end of all their troubles, and he would say that it was true, marriage is the end of trouble, but it's the front end!

People had said Christine must be having twins because she was so big, and a doctor there confirmed it. In February the boys were born twenty days early, at San Antonio Baptist Hospital, on their aunt Libby's 27th birthday and they were identical. John Clayton and Joseph Layton Knopp were healthy and hungry. Christine didn't know that a woman could nurse two babies, but she did, and she also gave them bottles in order to satisfy them, because they always seemed to be hungry those first few months. One night, Paul woke her and the babies were crying. He asked her if she was going to feed them, and his voice sounded a little desperate. Christine said, "Sure, how long have they been crying?" He told her it had been about an hour and a half. She was so tired that she had slept right through it all! After the twins were six weeks old, she weaned them to the bottle entirely to be sure they were getting enough nutrients. They did sleep better and seem more satisfied after that.

Soon afterwards, they went back to Virginia for a visit. They put the twins into a basket next to the door on the front seat of the car, facing in opposite directions. Libby went along with them to help out and to see her family in Staunton. They stopped in Somerset, Kentucky to visit Christine's family, and Libby was able to meet all of them.

Once Christine was at a gathering of ladies and the twins had started to pull up on the furniture and walk by holding onto it. They were pulling up on her legs and stepping on her feet as they held onto her skirt. One lady remarked, "They'll step on your toes now, and on your heart later." Christine had heard that saying before, and she replied,

"I don't believe that saying. I believe that I can trust God with their future." This statement of faith had not been thought out, but had just come welling up from the depths of her being. That thought often came back to her as the boys grew up.

Chapter Four

P AUL'S HEALTH HAD been pretty good, but now he had a severe asthma attack. A pastor there suggested that Paul drive out to Prescott, Arizona to see if the weather would give him relief. Paul left on a Saturday in May 1950, and Christine was squeezing fresh orange juice for him, since they had read that vitamin C would help him. He drove 1200 miles alone, but as soon as he got there, he got a call that his third son was born so he started driving back. David Wesley was born fifteen months and sixteen days after John and Joseph. Paul tells of these events in his own words in a testimony entitled "How I overcame fear and worry":

"In the spring of 1950, my wife, twin boys and I were living in San Antonio, Texas. We had moved from Kentucky- where I had pastored a small church – to Texas on account of my health. Since the age of twelve I have suffered from asthma. I know what it is to spend many sleepless nights gasping for breath. After moving to Texas I got temporary relief, but the long hours of selling Fuller brushes together with the restless nights, I got to the end of myself. In desperation I made a trip to Arizona seeking a place to live where I would be free from the terrible malady. My wife and fifteen-month-old twins were left in San Antonio. Scarcely had I gotten to Prescott, Arizona, when word arrived telling of the birth of our third son. So I rushed back to Texas. We just didn't know what to do. It seemed to me that we must leave San Antonio but we had no "green light" to go to Arizona. Finally I was able to commit it all to God in faith, knowing that He would work it out. An inward peace came. In a few weeks we received a call to take a pastorate in the panhandle of Oklahoma and freedom from asthma followed. Now, whenever the petty worries of life come, I just say to myself, 'Look here, Paul! You have a GREAT problem. It's too great for you to handle. I look in the mirror and laugh and commit it all to Him.' "

In June at a camp meeting, a pastor asked if he'd be willing to pastor a church in Griggs, Oklahoma. Paul went there and preached and moved there with his family when David was nine weeks old. This was a very rural area. It had a post office, a general store, and a gas station. The family that ran the gas station lived in the back. The parsonage was fairly new. Paul felt really good and did a lot of work with a local farmer, John Elliot.

The twins had their own language and would jabber away to each other. They slept together in a large crib. They seemed to understand each other, even though no one else knew what they were saying. Pregnant again, Christine found out in December that she was carrying twins again. In February, Christine's younger sister Josephine had come to stay with them and to help with the older children when the twins were born. The doctor had told Christine not to do much bending since he was concerned she might rupture. Josephine was 20, and they introduced her to Bearl Elliot, an unmarried twin brother to the farmer that Paul had been working with. Bearl was 36 when they met. Josephine stayed until July 4, and then Bearl drove her to the train station. She took John and Joseph to Kentucky with her for a visit. In October, Bearl went to Kentucky and asked her father for her hand in marriage. He consented, and they got married, so Jo came back to Oklahoma to live.

Once Paul was away and Christine took the three boys to the barn to milk the cow. When they headed back to the house, the wind had risen, and Christine told the twins to hold tight to her skirts, while she carried the bucket of milk and the baby. She was afraid the barn door would prove too much for her, being so loaded down, but they made it to the house. Later they learned that the wind had been seventy miles per hour that day!

Christine's stomach swelled bigger and bigger, and she began to rub cocoa butter on it every day, because the skin was stretched so thin, it seemed it might burst. Soon she was getting so big that she thought she would have triplets! The doctor could only find one heartbeat, so he wanted to do an X-ray to be sure the twins weren't conjoined. The X-ray showed they were separate and in a head-down position, ready to be born. They drove to Guymon, Oklahoma the next day, and Christine's water broke, so Paul took her to the hospital. Finally, when she felt she couldn't make it another day, the identical twins were born in March, 1952. They were big healthy boys, and weighed a total of fourteen pounds. They named them Thomas Harry and Timothy Larry Knopp, and now their family had grown to a total of five.

One day, they drove up from being out, and a coyote was standing on its hind legs sniffing the barrel they burned trash in. That was a fun experience for all of them, to see a wild animal up close like that. It was always very windy there, and once the wind blew Russian thistle against a wire and board fence, then blew the sandy soil over it, all the way to the top of the fence. The thistles there were like tumbleweeds. They got goggles for the boys so they could play outside and the sand wouldn't get in their eyes. They also bought them little pilot's caps like the barnstormer pilots wore. Dust seeped in and spread throughout the house, so Christine put towels at the base of the doors to try to keep the blowing dust out.

Many of the homes and other buildings in Griggs were built mostly underground, with a row of windows around the top to allow light inside. The church was built that way, and one time the wind blew sand and it piled up against the windows. The men had to get shovels and clear the windows. They heated the church with coal. Once a big piece of coal rolled off of a stack and hit Paul's toe. He was thinking that his toe hurt really badly, but the rest of his body wasn't scolding his toe and saying, "That's just what you deserved." It came to him that in the body of Christ, we need to be the same, to sympathize with one another's weaknesses and sufferings rather than judging others and thinking it's their fault when they suffer. Just as the rest of the body yearns to relieve the suffering of an injured toe, so the members of the body of Christ should yearn to help whenever a member is hurting. That relieved Paul of the "burden" of being just one man as pastor of the church, though there were many needs and demands on his time.

Albert and Hermine Yahnig, Christine's brother and his wife who lived in Kentucky, came to visit in Griggs along with their son Stephen. They went out with Paul to hang clothes on the clothesline. Albert laughed and said it was really funny how they could hang up diapers and go back to the beginning and start taking down the ones they hung up first. They were already dry because it was so windy and dry there in Oklahoma.

After David could walk, around 1953, a hailstorm came up. Paul was out driving a tractor for a farmer as it was getting dark. He saw two storms coming toward each other and knew something unusual was coming. He put the tractor in the barn and got in the car to drive home. A hailstorm hit hard and fast, and broke the windshield of the car in several places. He stopped the car and climbed in the back seat. Eventually, the storm subsided and another car drove by, so he assumed it would be safe to drive home. When he reached home, several windows in the house had broken and glass was scattered across the floor. Christine had taken the boys to the basement, but they were crying from fear. They were very happy and relieved to see Paul come home safe. Another time, a lightning bolt hit Paul's wallet while he was in the house, and welded the clasp together. The electricity turned off in the house at the same time due to the storm. This was such a surprise to him, since storms in Virginia had never done such things to him.

Their next-door neighbor, John Elliot, Bearl's older brother, owned a store and he was the postmaster as well. When their Papa would take them to this store, the boys would always ask for a soda pop. Papa always said no because he didn't want to spend their grocery money on junk food. Sometimes John Elliot would give them each one, and it was so cold and such a treat. He also gave them a baby pig to raise. The boys raised and sold it. With the money they bought striped coveralls, leather caps, and goggles. Outfitted this way, people thought John, Joseph, and David were triplets. The boys would find John Elliot wherever he was in the store, but they weren't allowed in the post office. There were Dutch doors leading to the postal area, though, and he would talk to them over it while he distributed the mail. The boys loved to go to the outside of the store as well, and watch men pump up the gasoline into a big clear gas cylinder that had the gallons measured off on top. Then they would pump it down into their trucks or cars or tractors. They called John and Joseph the "why boys" because they asked so many questions about what the men were doing. One thing the boys noticed about John Elliot was that he always looked like he was sleeping in church because he kept his eyes closed. Afterwards, however, he would comment on the sermon and knew all about it.

One day, Paul came home from work in an airplane. He had been working for a man at a nearby farm. The farmer asked him to drive a tractor to Goodwill, Oklahoma. Paul was driving it down the road and all of a sudden he felt something give, the tractor tilted to one side, and to his astonishment he saw a big wheel roll by him down the road and into the field! The tractor stopped where it was. He used another farmer's telephone and called the owner of the tractor, who came to pick him up in his airplane. He flew a small Piper, and carried Paul the 18 or 20 miles home. It was a summer evening, still light, and the boys were flabbergasted to see their Papa land in an airplane right in front of the house!

One winter, the three older boys went out to play in deep snow. There was a crust on top because it had sleeted on top of the snowfall, and they could walk on it. John's foot broke through near a fence where it had drifted and he couldn't pull his leg back out. John said, "Go get Mama and Papa." Joseph lay down, told David to hold on to him, pulled John out, and then they went and told their parents about it.

Every Sunday, the boys wanted to invite people from church over for lunch. They loved to have company, but they were also hoping that their parents would forget what they had done at church. Mama would tell the boys they would get a spanking from Papa when they got home. They were always getting in trouble at church. They crawled on the floor under the pews during the sermon, and ladies were upset to look down and see them underneath everyone. The church was built partly underground and the roof was easy to climb up on, so after the service the boys went straight up there, even though they weren't supposed to. Also, there were stairs leading to the church basement and there was a narrow ledge, about six inches, that got higher and higher as you went down the stairs. They would jump down from the ledge, and again the ladies were upset and told on them. If company came over after church, the boys were able to eat and play outside with the kids and by late afternoon when the company went home, Mama would have "forgotten" to tell Papa about their naughtiness at church and that they needed a spanking. The boys loved to have company on Sundays.

A neighbor had a big bull. It was a Brangus bull, a cross between a Brahmin and Angus breed, and he was meanness personified. The boys often went in the field, but one day they had a friend with them and they went into an empty barn. They told the visiting kid that they could make a rattlesnake rattle. There was a nest of rattlers under the floorboards, and they jumped on the boards to disturb the snakes and make them shake their rattles. When they were heading back home across the field, the bull came after them, and they ran with all the speed they could muster. John, Joseph, and David dove through the fence, followed by their friend, with the bull only about five feet behind. Later the boy said he had such a good time with the Knopps, and would love to go play with them anytime!

Papa and Mama got some chickens and raised them. One grew into a mean rooster. He would fly up and grab one of the boys on the rear end, then peck him in the back of the head. He often drew blood. They hated it, of course, and complained to Papa. Papa said if he did it one more time, he would chop off his head. He did it again the next day, and Papa chopped off his head with a hatchet on a log. Usually when chickens were beheaded, they would run around in circles and then flop over, but this rooster ran in a straight line out through a field for about 25 yards, then fell over.

The church that Paul was pastoring in Oklahoma had problems, and the members were bickering among themselves. Some of the members didn't want to pay a tithe to the church, but Paul was tithing out of his salary. The church elders told him he didn't need to tithe from his salary. They were concerned because his family didn't have enough to eat. Paul and Christine prayed with the boys sometimes for food and then they would find that neighbors had left food on their doorstep. Paul was working at any other jobs he could find to earn extra money. Finally, when he prayed, the Lord spoke to him and said, "Young man, you've tried to serve me for many years. Now let me show you what I can do." Soon after this, he was offered a pastorate in Kansas and accepted it.

Paul holding John & Christine holding Joseph, 1949

Joseph and John in goggles, David

Joseph, Timothy, Thomas, & John, Mama, David, Papa

Stephen, Mark Thomas, David, Timothy, John,
Mama holding Daniel, Papa holding Nathan, Joseph

Thomas, Timothy with Nathan, Mark John,
David, Joseph, Mama holding Daniel, Papa, Stephen

Stephen, Nathan, Daniel Mark, Papa, Mama, John, Thomas, Timothy, Joseph

Stephen, Mark, Papa, Mama, Nathan, Daniel,
Thomas, John, David, Joseph, Timothy

Marilyn, Mama, Papa, Anne, Barbara, David, Stephen, Joseph,
John, Timothy, Thomas

Paul, Andrew, Michael, Anne, John, Isaac

Caleb, Nina, Aaron, Peter, Joseph, Zach

Marilyn holding Nathanael, Samuel, David, Joel, Joy

Ben, Christy, Tristan, Thomas, Wes, Barbara, Melissa, Emily, Laura

Jonathan, Timothy, Anne, Hannah

Elijah, Keziah, Isaiah, Andrea (Sissy), Mark

Stephen

Karen, Brittany, Asher, Kaitlin, Hunter, & Nathan

Linda & Daniel

Chapter Five

P AUL AND CHRISTINE had lived in Griggs for four years. Now they moved to Kinsley, Kansas in August 1954 to pastor a church there. It took a whole day for the family to get packed. Christine drove the family car and Paul drove a truck to accommodate their growing family and possessions. Paul said Christine fell asleep at the wheel several times and weaved on the road. They drove all night until about 2:00 AM. They arrived on September 1 at midnight, and Christine said she was so sleepy on the trip that it was quite scary. She rolled the car window down and the fresh air helped a little. It was a great relief to reach their new home and fall into bed. Some of the ladies from the church had worked very hard to get their new home ready for them, but there were no sheets on the boys' beds, so they spread a quilt on the floor and the five boys slept there. In Griggs it had always cooled down at night, but in Kinsley in August, it didn't. That was hard to adjust to, and to get back into a healthy sleep pattern.

The boys started to school and Paul drove the school bus. One week, he was the janitor at Northside Elementary, and the next week he filled in as principal when the principal had to be away. He sometimes worked three or four jobs just to make ends meet, since the small pastorate didn't pay much. Christine read about edible wild plants, and she began to pick and cook wild greens from the yard and fields. One kind they liked was called lamb's quarters, and it helped to fill everyone's stomachs. They always had a large vegetable garden in the summer and grew a variety of vegetables, and she canned and froze all that they couldn't eat.

One time, when Christine's father had come to visit in Kinsley, Paul and Christine went to a church function and left him to babysit for the boys. By this time, the older twins were about six years old. "Pop" fell asleep in a chair in the living room and started to snore. The boys went quietly out of the house and turned on a hose, using it to thoroughly wet the porch floor. Then they started sliding across the porch. Soon they were having so much fun they forgot to be quiet, and Pop woke up. He came out onto the porch and wanted to be angry with them, but he found that he just couldn't because he was laughing too hard.

Each summer the family attended a camp meeting in Wichita, Kansas, and Paul did a lot of work with the youth there. Paul served as an evangelist sometimes and sometimes he would sing solos. One time, Christine accompanied him there to a youth leaders' overnight conference. A youth leader there taught them to cook an egg either in an orange rind or an orange juice can, over a campfire. His point was that experience is the best teacher. Some of the eggs went in the fire, but some were fit to eat. Another time, they had gone to Guymon, Oklahoma, and saw a man demonstrating how to use a kitchen appliance to pulverize eggshells and use them in cooking. When they got home, they thought they'd try putting some whole eggs in pancakes for the nutritional value. Their mixer didn't grind the shells as fine as in the demonstration, however, and no one particularly favored the extra crunch in the pancakes, so they agreed to let that be a one- time experiment.

Christine had suspected that she was pregnant when they moved to Kinsley and soon realized it was true. She had a miscarriage during the night one night. The family doctor came the next morning at 8:00. She was only about two months into the pregnancy, and he didn't call it a miscarriage, but it surely was, about two months along. He said she was fine and nothing would be wrong with having more children. She talked to the older boys, and told them that there must have been something wrong with the baby all along. She explained that the baby had been growing inside her, but sometimes there is something wrong and God takes a baby to him before it's born. She said it was sad, but it would be okay, because they still had each other. Since the baby was so young, they didn't have a funeral. Soon she discovered that she was pregnant again, and this time she carried the baby to full term. Mark Allen was born in December of 1955, and now they were a family of eight.

There was a park across the street for the boys to play in, and their parents would flip the porch lights on and off when it was time to come in. A tornado sent them to the basement one time. Paul was working at Al's Clothing Store, and he and some other men went outside and watched the tornado circling around the town. An old Indian saying was that a tornado would never hit Kinsley because of the way the river circled the town. It tore up about seven miles in its path that day, but it didn't come into the town.

When John and Joseph were in first grade, they were coming home with their papers all marked up with red pen. Christine went to the school and talked with the teacher and found that they were misunderstanding the directions involving color. She had them sort knives, forks and spoons of different colors, and then they were fine in school. When Mark was about six months old, they moved to another house at 501 East 8th Street. Christine was pregnant again, and Stephen Paul was born in January of 1957.

The church they were pastoring there was small with only about fifty members. Paul enjoyed it and the people were happy with him. He saw the "church universal" in Isaiah in his studies and preached that all of God's people were one. An older man in the church who had been a minister gave Paul a chart he had made of men in the Bible. It was very interesting and extensive. That same man had a granddaughter who babysat for the Knopp boys sometimes.

The family didn't own a television and they didn't go to amusement parks or movie theaters, but the boys were never bored. They had each other to play with, aided by their active imaginations. They liked to pretend they were railroad owners, and named such giants as the Santa Fe Railroad and the Pacific and Western. The train ran right through the middle of their little town, and they loved to go to the station and watch trains arrive, passengers get off and on, and fuel and cargo get loaded. Other times they pretended to own big tractor manufacturing companies like John Deere and Case. In the summer they went out of town to the riverbed they called the "Our Kansas" river, which would dry up to not much more than a little trickle. It provided many hours of joy for them as they dug and splashed in it.

The boys would sometimes use the neighbor kids as guinea pigs to try things they wouldn't do themselves. One time they got the idea of having someone jump off the roof of the house into a blanket with the boys holding tight to the edges, like firemen. They were afraid to jump themselves, so they persuaded a neighbor boy to do it. He jumped, and the force of his weight pulled the blanket right out of their hands. He hit the ground with a thud.

But then he got up, fussing loudly. "I thought you guys were going to hold the blanket!" he protested. They said they were sorry, that if he tried again, they would hold tighter, and they felt sure that he'd be safe this time. They finally persuaded him to try it again, but the same thing happened the second time, and that game was abandoned.

It was a busy time of life. Christine was nursing Stephen, and taking care of six older boys. Mark was only a toddler at the time. She weaned Stephen to a bottle, but started noticing that the bottle was empty very fast, and it seemed that he couldn't have drunk it that fast. So she started paying closer attention, and discovered that Mark was getting the bottle away from his baby brother and draining it. She had to pay close attention to them after that to be sure that Stephen got enough milk.

Two years later on September 1959, Nathan Albert was born, and now there were ten in the family. They still lived in the same large house on Eighth Street, with a wrap-around porch and a big grassy yard. This was unusual since the boys were apt to wear down the grass at any house they lived until they were playing in the dirt. One year, they didn't travel to Staunton to visit Paul's family, and instead Paul put in a large concrete area in the back yard with a clothesline mounted on it. They let the boys dig a deep hole in the back yard that they called "the foxhole", and they spent hours playing down in that hole. The soil was pretty sandy and easy to dig. Their parents thought as long as they knew where they were and what they were doing, there was no need to worry, and they were allowed a lot of freedom. One night, they wanted to spend the night in the hole. Their parents said they could, but they should feel free to come in at any time if they wanted to. Mama left the back door light on for them. Mark was with his brothers, but he was only about 4 years old at the time, and he went on in to bed first. The rest of the boys stayed out there until about 2:30 in the morning, and then they were cold and came inside to their warm beds.

Once, Papa and Mama received a bill that they had no funds to cover. Papa brought it up at the supper table and prayed with the family that God would provide the money. He didn't mention it to anyone else. The next day, a check for the exact amount to pay the bill was left in their door. Papa told Mama and the boys and they rejoiced.

One Sunday afternoon when John was about ten years old, he got left at home when the family went on an outing. He was in the bathroom and everyone jumped in the car and left, so when he came out, no one was home. They had been invited to the home of a family from their church for a picnic about thirty miles away. Mama called him when they reached the people's house

and apologized, but she said they were too far away to come back and get him. She told him to fix himself a peanut butter sandwich for supper, so he did and just sat on the porch steps and waited for them to come home. It was very quiet around the house that day without the rest of the family.

While visiting in Oklahoma, the boys were crossing a fence and saw a rattlesnake. They ran inside and told their Aunt Josephine. She came out with a gun and shot the snake, and the boys were very impressed. They had never seen a woman handle a gun, especially not their aunt! Back in Kinsley, the family was gaining a reputation because they had so many boys. Once the five older boys played on the same basketball team, and the newspaper reported that it was a team of Knopps.

Chapter Six

DANIEL WAS BORN in August 1961, and Mama and Papa had a hard time choosing a middle name for him. Finally they settled on George, after Paul's father. When Daniel was nine months old, the family moved to Virginia, and lived for a time in Paul's parents' basement apartment. This was step of faith for Paul, since his asthma was usually worse in the Shenandoah Valley. He felt the leading of the Holy Spirit to move, so they packed up and went to Virginia. The boys had always loved visiting their grandparents in Virginia, so they were delighted! Grandpa George offered to help out with the boys or the chores. He incorporated some of the older boys into his work. He was a master carpenter and very talented in his work. He was especially skilled at curved staircases, and a number of the historic homeowners in Staunton hired him to add one to their homes. He also gave Christine a cast iron skillet for frying chicken. Paul's mother sometimes brought bacon downstairs to him, since she knew he loved it. Christine noticed that she didn't bring any for the rest of the family, but only to him. It would have been difficult to divide it into eleven equal pieces, which was what she normally did with any special treats. She said later that she figured her mother-in-law didn't have enough bacon to feed all eleven of them, and didn't think that the rest of them would mind their Papa having bacon with his breakfast.

Papa and the older boys often walked from Grandpa's house to Oak Grove chapel on Middlebrook road, where some members of the family had been attending services and wanted Paul to come as their pastor. This was about a three mile walk. One day, Papa asked John and Joseph if they had ever noticed a property along the road that looked abandoned. Papa called Dick Firebaugh, a local realtor. He said he would look into it. Papa said all he could afford to pay was $10,000. It was owned by a group; Firebaugh asked the owners and they all wanted to sell for that price. So he borrowed the money. There was an old house on the property which the boys helped renovate, and the total cost of the renovation, including replacing most of the floors, was around

$1,100. The property included thirty acres of woods behind the house. They moved into the house on Middlebrook road in 1965.

On April 28, the day they moved, Christine got a call from her brother in Kentucky, and he told her that her father had passed away that day. She and Paul flew to London, Kentucky from a small airport in Weyers Cave to attend the funeral, and her brother Albert picked them up.. Her mother had died eleven years earlier, and though she missed her Pop, it was good just to be with her four brothers and two sisters and their families. Paul's brother Jimmy and his wife Jane Anne took care of their boys, and since they had a large family themselves, the boys enjoyed being with them. When Paul and Christine flew back in from Kentucky to Weyers Cave, a man Paul knew from a CO camp and his daughter came up to them at the little airport. The man had heard they were flying in and came to meet them, but Paul and Christine didn't know that. They pretended that he had come to meet them and pick them up, and, lo and behold, he had! He and Paul reminisced about their days together during the war.

There was a barn next to the house on Middlebrook, and John at 14 bought a calf and raised it. They had a neighbor boy named Leroy who came to visit every day. He liked playing with all the Knopp boys. He was very independent and rode his bike all over town. He was usually dirty, and he often showed up at meal time. One day, Leroy came into the house crying with a hoof print on his bare chest.

He said, "Your cow kicked me!" When Mama asked him why he thought the cow had kicked him, he said probably because he was hitting it with a stick. She suggested that he not do that again.

One night, Papa and Mama and the five older boys went to a Full Gospel meeting at Ingleside in Staunton, and Mark and Diane Yasuhara, a Hawaiian couple, were ministering and singing. The singing was beautiful, and afterwards they went up front to tell them how much they had enjoyed it.

Mark had a big grin, and when he saw the five boys, he said, "I think that what you need is a few more boys!" Mama told him they had four more boys at home.

His eyes got big, and he said, "I was only joking!" Then he said, "Maybe I could come out there tomorrow and get my hands in the dirt." That was the beginning of a long and joyful friendship. Whenever the Hawaiians were in the area, Papa and Mama always invited them to come and stay in their home.

In February 1970 their family was invited by a man named Jim White to Richmond for an Ashram, which was a prayer meeting that usually lasted for a night and a day. Papa took the older boys and went to it, and Mama stayed home with the younger ones. She had always loved to go places and meet new people, and she would have preferred to go this time, but as she was reading the Bible, the Lord directed her to Isaiah 54:1-2. "Sing, O barren woman, you who were never in labor; because more are the children of the desolate woman than of her who has a husband." Christine put down her Bible and asked, "Lord, why do you call me barren? I have nine boys!" The Lord told her to read on, that he was talking about spiritual children. So she read, "Enlarge the place of your tent, stretch your tent curtains wide, do not hold back; lengthen your cords, strengthen your stakes. For you will spread out to the right and to the left; your descendants will dispossess nations and settle in their desolate cities."

As she mused on these verses, she realized that God was planning to do something special in their home, and she needed to be ready. She also remembered reading in the Old Testament stories of King David that one time he left some men at home to guard their camp when he went to war. He and the soldiers brought home great riches as the spoils of war, and his soldiers at first did not want to share them with the men who had stayed home, saying that they didn't participate in the victory. But David said to divide the loot equally with those who stayed behind because their service had enabled them to fight and they deserved it just as much as those who had gone out. Christine realized that God would bless her and speak to her at home as well as when she went to meetings.

Many of their extended family and friends were attending the services at the little chapel. Papa had gotten involved with a group called Full Gospel Businessmen through a neighbor who was a dentist, Fulton Gilbert, who first invited him to a Full Gospel dinner in nearby

Harrisonburg. The goal of the Full Gospel Businessmen's organization was to help the Body of Christ, his church, to discover what it meant to be filled with the Holy Spirit and to see lives and churches transformed in the process. Because of his involvement with that organization, Paul lost most of his congregation at the chapel. One Sunday a visiting speaker talked of the gifts of the Spirit, including speaking in heavenly tongues. He prayed for specific people who asked to receive the baptism in the Holy Spirit, and to speak in tongues. The Full Gospel teaching that there was an additional gift of the infilling of the Holy Spirit did not agree with the teachings of many denominations, and those who disagreed left and most of them did not return for services at the little chapel. The family continued to hold the services, and Paul's mother Bessie still attended every week.

The day after that meeting at the chapel, the Gilbert family, who lived close to the Knopps, invited them over to hear the man speak again at their house. He prayed for Christine this time, and when he asked what she wanted God to do for her, she said she wanted to be a better wife, a better mother, and a better Christian.

"You want it all, eh?" He laid his hands on her shoulders and prayed, and she began to feel laughter bubbling up from deep inside. It was such a wonderful, joyous laughter that she couldn't contain it, and it began to come out. She giggled and shook and laughed and laughed, and finally, Fulton sat down beside her on the bench she was sitting on, and said, "Oh Christine, I want some of that!"

In January 1971 a big snowstorm forced the family to stay at home on Sunday, and they had church at home for three weeks. Papa heard God speak to him through the Holy Spirit and say, "You've been trying to serve me; now let me show you what I can do."

Papa told the family, "I just want to know Him more. Jesus said in his prayer before He was crucified, 'This is real life, to know the only true God, and Jesus Christ, whom you have sent.' Jesus prayed for us that we would be one with God as he and His father are one. He promises us eternal life, righteousness, peace, and joy in the Holy Spirit. The scripture says, "Be joyful always, pray continually, and give thanks in all circumstances, for this is the will of God for you in Christ Jesus."

Mama's favorite Bible verse is Romans 8:28, "And we know that all things work together for good for those who love Him and are called according to His purpose." Another favorite is Psalm 46:1 and 10. "God is our refuge and strength, a very present help in time of trouble", and "Be still and know that I am God." Papa said it makes life much easier to serve God because he takes care of all our needs and we don't have to worry. Jesus said to seek first his kingdom and all these things will be added to you. Sometimes we may feel barren and unfruitful but it's just because it can take time to bear the fruit of the Spirit. Papa's advice is "to seek God with all your heart. The Bible says the kingdom of God is like treasure that a man found in a field and sold all he had to buy that field. Serving God is the most important thing in life. If we miss that, we miss everything. Jesus told about the seed falling in different places and not being fruitful. Seek God in all the decisions of life, and especially in marriage. People who get married and then find themselves unhappy need to bring God into their marriage and seek Him. It pays to serve God regardless of how much trouble it causes you."

Chapter Seven

A S THE FAMILY worshipped at home, it seemed best to them to have the services there at the big farmhouse on Middlebrook Road instead of going back to the chapel. People began to join them. Paul's mother Bessie was always there and Paul drove in to pick her up on Sunday mornings. She stayed after the worship time for Sunday lunch, along with anyone else who was attending. A woman from Arlington, Virginia named Addie Chegwin called, saying that a friend had told her if she ever came to Staunton to be sure and look up the Knopp family with nine boys. She brought some college students to visit, and began to visit them every weekend. She had met a couple named Frank and Wendy Wilbur when Frank had been the speaker at a Full Gospel meeting in Charlottesville. Frank was a biology professor at Mary Baldwin College in Staunton, and he was teaching a Sunday school class at Second Presbyterian church. Addie suggested that he bring his Sunday school class out to meet the Knopp family, and so he did. Two of the girls in the class were Mary Baldwin students, Susan Jones and Susan Vandeventer, and they began to attend the services at the Knopp's house on Sunday evenings. Addie taught them all some scripture songs she knew, and the Sunday night meetings were mainly for singing.

Frank attended a Sunday night meeting for the first time in May 1971, and he brought two students from Washington and Lee University. Ben Smith and Austin McGaskill. The first time they came, there were twelve people there. By September, there were over 24 people and the group moved from the living room to the kitchen. By late 1972 the group meeting in the kitchen had grown to over 125 people, including many college students and adults, as well as some high school students. Also in 1972, Sunday morning services with many visitors to the home began.

The word seemed to spread fast about those meetings, because students from James Madison and Washington and Lee universities began to come, as well as more Mary Baldwin students. People were excited about the Holy Spirit and the power displayed during the Charismatic Renewal. People were becoming Christians, getting filled with the Spirit and speaking in tongues, getting miraculously healed of physical problems, and finding new meaning in life. Several young men who needed a place to stay moved in with the Knopps, and their home became quite busy and full of activity.

Addie Chegwin gave Christine a guest book to record people's names and contact information, and Christine had everyone sign it when they came for the first time.

"Why don't we get some fried chicken and have lunch for everyone who comes for the services on Sunday mornings?" Addie asked. Mama made her own bread from wheat that she ground in a flour mill, so she served that along with peanut butter and honey, which was the way the family liked to eat it. She cooked a big batch of potatoes and the boys helped her mash them. Soon people began to bring other dishes to go along with Mama's basic meat, potatoes, and bread. In February 1973, Steve Timberlake, who was an attorney in Staunton and had been attending on Sunday nights, told Paul he had $1,000 for him to add on to the house to accommodate the extra people. The meetings had become quite crowded, and spilled over from the kitchen into the living room. So Paul and the boys began working on an addition to the house. They drew up a plan for an addition of a large room on the main floor and four bedrooms upstairs. John, Joseph, Thomas, Timothy, Mark and Stephen had been sleeping in the basement on foam pads in order to accommodate the guests they had living in the house. The extra bedrooms would come in handy.

Mama still loved to go places and meet people, but as she stayed at home, people began to come to the Knopp home more and more. She was already doing the laundry, cooking the meals, and washing dishes constantly. She delegated some work to the boys, but she still did the largest share of the housework, especially cooking and cleaning up the kitchen. On Sundays, everyone who came to church was invited to stay for lunch. Mama cooked most of the food for these meals. The people who attended regularly brought food and some of them helped clean up. There was still a lot of work to do, and Mama was always working hard. She spent a lot of time praying while working at the sink. Most people who knew her remember her best at the kitchen sink, where she could often be heard to say, "Thank you, Jesus!"

Papa and Mama had prayed to have only boys after David was born. One time Mama was in downtown Staunton on Beverley Street and heard a group of girls calling out to her, "Mama, Mama!" She was surprised and delighted to hear girls calling her Mama and then they ran up and gave her a hug. People sometimes asked Mama how they could tell the twins apart. She would say that she could tell them apart because she knew them.

One time, Thomas asked Mama, "There's something I've always wondered about. How do you know I'm Thomas? Am I really Timothy?"

"No!" she said in a voice that allowed no argument. Mama told him she left the twins' hospital IDs on until she knew them so well there was no more question.

In MArch of 1973, they all began to work on the addition on evenings and weekends. First they began digging the foundation, and they found there was a huge rock in the area they needed to excavate. It presented quite a challenge, and blasting was involved, but after that was done, the addition quickly took shape, and others from the church came by to lend a hand. By early 1974, it was finished, and after that, the church had plenty of space. The family also had plenty of space, and the boys were able to move upstairs, and although the four twins still shared a room, they now had beds, and they were much more comfortable.

Baptisms were held in the river on Paul's brother Jimmy's farm. The river had a slippery, rocky, uneven bottom. Once when Papa went in to baptize someone, he slipped under when he last his footing, and one of his sons had to help him get to shore.

The church was still growing, and the Sunday night services were especially popular, drawing many young people, and also people from many other churches enjoyed the singing, since it was primarily a worship service. One lady, Mrs. Archer Tullidge, was a member of a big church in town, but she said she felt closer to Heaven at the Knopp's house on Sunday nights than any other time in her life. Sometimes, as the worship took place on Sunday nights, it sounded like angels were joining in the singing. An elderly couple in Staunton, Hal and Helen Wallace, attended the Sunday night services, and one day Helen said that the Lord had given her a desire to meet with the Mary Baldwin girls. She held several Bible studies with them, and taught them about what the Bible had to say to young women, wives, and mothers. Frank and Wendy Wilbur began to have Bible studies in their home in town, because with all the young Christians, especially at Mary Baldwin, Frank felt that they needed to know the teachings of the Bible. He was a gifted teacher, and the Knopps attended the meetings as well. Sometimes, some of the other nearby college students also came to the meetings. At times, there was special prayer afterwards for people to know Christ or to be healed, and once a young man was instantly healed of a broken arm! That same night, several girls said they experienced some kind of heavenly visitation as they walked back to Mary Baldwin, and they fell down on the sidewalk, overcome with awe.

The Charismatic Renewal was happening all over the world, and they read books and heard testimonies from visitors of God's miracles in many other places as well. Often after supper, Papa would either read several chapters of the Bible, or read from another Christian book. He read about Jim Elliot giving his life in Ecuador in order to evangelize the Auca Indians, and about miracles in Indonesia in *Like a Mighty Wind* by Mel Tari. He also read the biographies of several Christian leaders like George Mueller and Smith Wigglesworth. Visitors were drawn to their home to listen to him and converse with him. Their home became a place for people from all walks of life to meet and find hope in Christ.

Students from local colleges began to attend the services at the Knopp home. James Madison University, Virginia Military Institute, Washington and Lee, Bridgewater College, and Mary Baldwin College were some of the schools they came from. On Sunday evenings they gathered in the spacious kitchen to sing scripture songs and choruses they had learned from other churches and revivals. Many people came from other churches to enter into the spirited worship and praise at these meetings. Fulton Gilbert began to attend with his wife and four children and they became close friends of the family. By this time, John and Joseph were attending Virginia Tech on a work-study scholarship, studying aerospace engineering. They would sometimes bring friends from school with them on weekends, so the house was always full of people.

The fellowship meetings were called the Knopp fellowship or just the Knopps. The number of people attending eventually outgrew the home, and the fellowship group met in several different locations. The name was changed to Community Fellowship Church, which now meets in the old city library building on South Market Street. Many of the Knopp family are still members, including Mama Knopp. She has always prayed for her family the same way her mother did. And she also prays for members of the church regularly.

In 1981, the church had decided to start a Christian school, and John Morrison taught the first classes in his basement. Since then, the school has grown considerably. Grace Christian elementary and middle schools are located across the street from Gypsy Hill Park. The high school occupies the building on Market Street. Grace Christian athletic center was built on land donated by Papa and Mama behind their home on Middlebrook Avenue.

"We're still seeing the effects of what God can do," Mama says.

The church has sent missionaries to Turkey, Albania, Africa, Syria, Lebanon, Israel, India, Nicaragua, Poland, Ukraine, Armenia, Nepal, and Japan, as well as many other countries. The church helped establish orphanages in Uganda, and two of the elders, Clay Sterrett and John Hagen, visited there and helped train over 10,000 church leaders. About 20 other church members have visited and ministered there. And Mama has over 11,000 signatures in her little book.

Papa often said that the Lord started this ministry, not him. The Lord brought the people, some of them just curious at first, but once they attended, they began to encounter God, and their lives were changed. Papa also said, "God has taken us into His family. I like eternal life and that's what He promised us. The Kingdom of God is righteousness, peace, and joy in the Holy Spirit. The Scripture says, 'Be joyful always, pray continually, and give thanks in all circumstances, for this is the will of God concerning you.' The Lord has taught me that what He's put into my hands is His property as well. In a sense, I'm a slave to God. To have a master like Him is a great thing because He will take care of all I need. Jesus said, 'Seek first His kingdom and righteousness and all these things will be added to you.' I hope I can be an encouragement to people. We've been blessed. We're still in love. We can look at nature and see God at work. Sometimes we feel barren, but just like the trees in winter still bring forth buds in spring that burst into bloom, your life will be fruitful again if you hang on and trust Him."

Before Papa died, the Lord spoke to Mama and said, "Christine, I'll take care of you." She thought she would die first and be better off if it happened that way. She is still seeing every day how well He is taking care of her. In the weeks before he died, Papa told many people that he would soon see Jesus. He also said this was what he had been looking for all his life. Paul Black Knopp went to his heavenly reward on November 17, 2008. He was almost 95.

Postscript:

Years have passed since the events of this story took place. Mama continues on strong, now 99, with a great memory, as well as keen eyesight and hearing. She goes to exercise in the pool at Augusta Fitness 5 or 6 times a week, and inspires everyone. She is still a prayer warrior. She now has 27 grandchildren and 37 great grandchildren. You may contact her at cmarieknopp@juno.com.

They were 10 days short of celebrating 61 years of marriage.

A note from Anne:

A number of people helped me in putting together this book. Papa and Mama themselves contributed most of the material. I used recordings of Papa's voice as well as writings of his. My husband, John, one of their nine sons, contributed in more ways than I can count, by sharing his memories and always believing in me. Their nine sons contributed their memories and helped with editing. Clay Sterrett, one of the elders at Community Fellowship Church, helped with editing. This book was a labor of love for me to write.

The Love Story of
Papa & Mama
Knopp